MW01063385

THE RULES

A GUIDE FOR PEOPLE OWNED BY CATS

INKBLOT BOOKS

VACAVILLE CA

The Rules
A Guide For People Owned By Cats

All Rights Reserved
© 2008 K.A. Thompson

No part of this book may be reproduced or transmitted in any form or by any means, without permission in writing from the publisher.

Published by Inkblot Books

Vacaville California

www.inkblotbooks.com

ISBN 978-932461-16-9

Printed in the United States of America

THE RULES
A GUIDE FOR PEOPLE OWNED BY CATS

MAX THOMPSON

Also by Max Thompson

The Psychokitty Speaks Out: Diary of a Mad Housecat

The Psychokitty Speaks Out: Something of Yours Will Meet A
Toothy Death

Visit Max online at his blog *The Psychokitty Speaks Out*
http://psychokitty.blogspot.com

Books one of his people wrote

Charybdis
As Simple As That
Finding Father Rabbit
It's Not About The Cookies

You'd look this grumpy, too, if you lived with my People.

INTRO

With my seventh birthday came a Holy Crapola moment: *I'm seven freaking years old!* My life may very well be half over. I'm middle aged, maybe even a senior kitty. I've met some kitties online who are pushing 20 years old—that's like 100 in people years.

Or 80.

Maybe 63.

Whatever. It's a lot. When I think of those kitties I feel pretty young, but there's this voice in the back of my head telling me I need to get done all the things I want to do, because, HOLY CARPOLY, my life might be HALF OVER.

It really bites when you think about it. People get 70 or 80 or even a hundred years on this planet, and if a cat gets 15, it's like, BONUS! Doood, you get two extra years! I think we deserve at least as much as our furless ~~staff~~ caregivers, although I suppose they need that extra time to get things right, what with all the thinking in circles that they do.

It's not all that complicated, People. You get up
every morning, eat, poop, stretch, nap, eat, look out the
window, eat, run around the house like your butt is on
fire, eat, poop again, and sleep some more. If someone
really bugs you, you either treat something of theirs to a
toothy death or poop on their pillow. How many years
do you really need to figure out the rest is all just a dis-
traction from enjoying the better things in life?

So kitties get fifteen or twenty years if they're really
lucky. We learn just about everything we need to learn in
the first two or three years (our Crackhead Kitty years, if
you will; you think it's funny but for the first six months
we really don't know why that THING has attached itself
to our butt, and you'd run around at top speed, too, if a
giant snake was sucking your life out through your ass...)
and then have the rest to enjoy the fruits of all that
learning we've done. Unfortunately, some of us live
outside, alone, enduring the hard life, but some of us
were lucky enough to get Forever Homes with people
who continually frustrate and baffle us. But hey, you buy
us enough Stinky Goodness, crunchy treats, kitty crack,
and other assorted toys, and we can tolerate you.

We'd tolerate you a little more if you'd clean out the
litter box a bit more frequently.

And face it, people, we make your lives better; we
make a difference in your world. What person's life is
truly complete without a little cat hair in their morning
cereal or some fine black fur on their nice white t-shirt?
I'm sure there are people out there who don't get it and
think their lives are just fine without a resident feline
advisor, but they know not of which they know not. If
they just knew how much better life would be if they had

a cat to watch over them, they'd be out there loading their grocery carts with the finest Stinky Goodness and Kitty Crack they could afford.

Oh yeah, if you're owned by a cat and you're buying that really cheap dry kibble at the dollar store, you are mean, and a herd of kitties needs to get together, pull your hair, and make you cry. Or poop on you. Whichever one would freak you out the most.

There's the rub. People just don't always know The Rules. They THINK they know how to care for a kitty, what to feed them, what toys they need, how much interaction and stimulation they should provide their kitty. But truly...people, you just don't get it.

When I had my 7th birthday Holy Crapoly epiphany, I also began to realize that one of the things I wanted to do with my remaining years was to make sure that people would finally get it. That they would come to understand how Real Life With Cats works; if I can make them understand, then life will be better for everyone.

Well, maybe not for dogs. Dogs can figure out how to get people to understand them on their own, although they seem to be simple enough creatures. Feed them, throw the ball, scoop their poop. I don't think they need much more.

There are just a few basic areas in which people need some guidance: the care and feeding of the kitty (on demand), sleeping rules (it's not your bed), bringing home another kitty (don't), when to provide a lap (on demand), toys, games, music appreciation, and language skills.

You can handle this, you really can.

Well, some of you can. The rest of you will continue to annoy your kitties, and things of yours will be pooped upon in frustration. Or things you like will be treated to a toothy death. There's no point in getting upset, because you likely deserve it.

On Feeding The Kitty

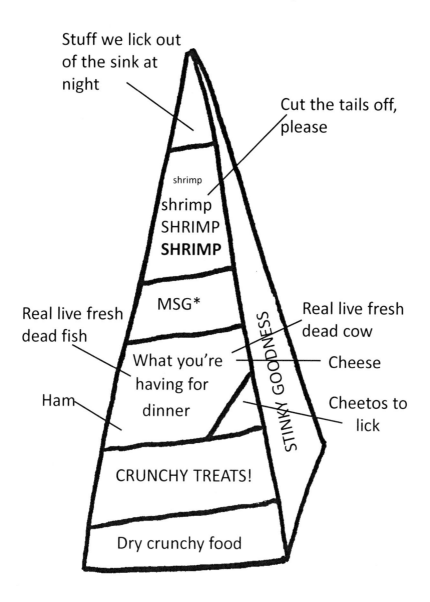

Stuff we lick out of the sink at night

Cut the tails off, please

shrimp
shrimp
SHRIMP
SHRIMP

MSG*

Real live fresh dead fish

Real live fresh dead cow

STINKY GOODNESS

Cheese

What you're having for dinner

Cheetos to lick

Ham

CRUNCHY TREATS!

Dry crunchy food

CAT FOOD PYRAMID
The Basis of Feline Nutritional Needs

*MSG = More Stinky Goodness

What Kitties Need

10 cans per day
Really
Would I lie?

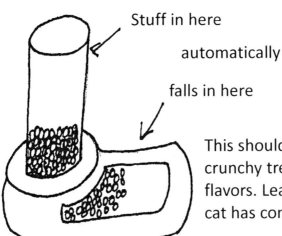

Stuff in here

automatically

falls in here

This should be filled with crunchy treats in various flavors. Leave where your cat has constant access.

Opened by primary food giver

Opened by non-feeder
THESE DON'T COUNT!!!

If someone other than the primary food giver opens a can of Stinky Goodness, it should not count as a meal. It is a snack, and the primary food giver should then feed the kitty more Stinky Goodness later in the day.

If you are not sitting at the table and you have food, it is acceptable for the kitty to stick his face into your edible business; if you don't want kitty help, eat at the table where he understands the #1 rule is No Sticking Your Face Into What The People Are Eating.

If you go hunting and bring home 50 cans of Stinky Goodness, it's not fair to stack them up in the cupboard and not give the kitty one of them. If the kitty sees you putting away the cans, it is your duty to open one for him. If there is another kitty and he doesn't hear it, it sucks to be him, but open a can for the observant and watchful kitty.

Counter. We get on them. Get over it.

The withholding of Stinky Goodness is a federal offense punishable by 3 years in prison.

I swear.

So give the kitty Stinky Goodness, and lots of it.

Kitties have birthdays, too. Make a cake for yourself and give the kitty some real live fresh dead shrimp.

There *must* be real live fresh dead shrimp on a kitty's birthday. And kitty crack. Without those two things it's not a Happy Birthday. A person can make the birthday even happier by adding some steak in there somewhere. Like in the cake. Shrimp and kitty crack and a cake made of steak. It's alliterative and munch-worthy all in one.

Fairness in Feeding

First kitty's food dish

Second kitty's food dish

You can have this if you want

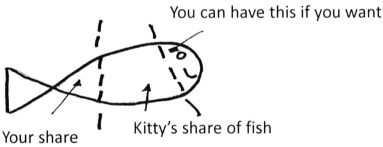

Your share
of fish

Kitty's share of fish

Ham

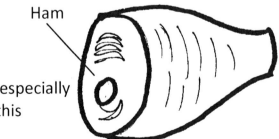

Meezer kitties especially
seem to need this

Note that the kitty is not on the table.
He's just curious. Don't get bent.

You

Your dinner

Kitty is just trying to
see what you have

If he is good and does not stick his face into your edible
business, give him a tiny taste. It's only polite.

You do want to be polite.

Right?

If your kitty eats dry food and any part of the bottom of his dry food dish is visible, do not mock the kitty when he requests that you add more food. Just do it. Visible food dish bottoms are highly distressing

Visible bottom

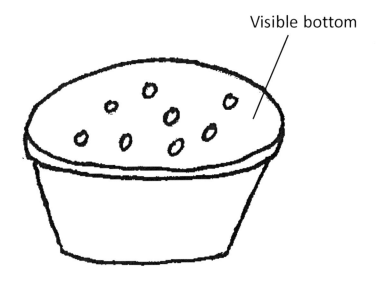

Fill the dish before the kitty has a heart attack

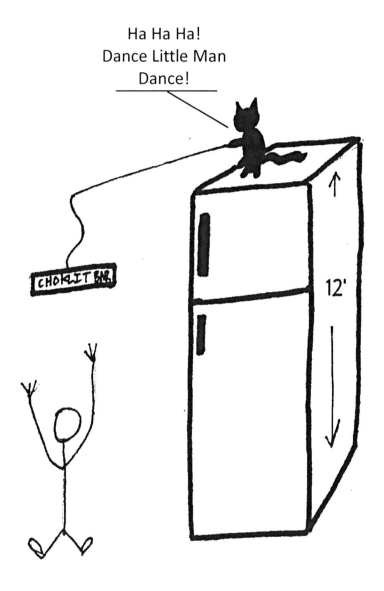

How would you like it if we made *you* dance for your treats?

Here is a blank page on which you may write notes.
Trust me. You need them.

Toys & Games: Things a kitty needs

The Climbing Tower

Prime place
from which a
kitty can barf

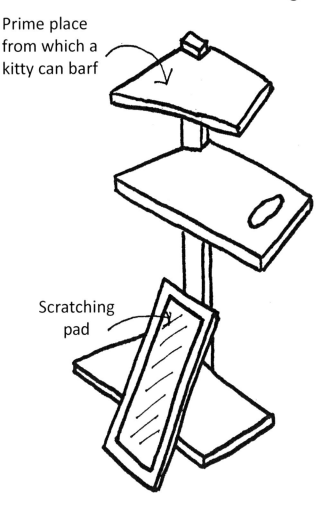

Scratching
pad

Every kitty needs at least one of these: a carpeted climb-ing tower. Or cat tree. Whatever you want to call it. The kitty won't care, as long as you get him one. Oh, and stick it in front of a window. Kitties like that.

If a person leaves anything out on a kitchen counter that can be rolled, spun, or battered around, it belongs to the kitty by default. This includes potatoes, bottle tops, and eggs, although eggs can typically only be played with for 2.41 seconds.

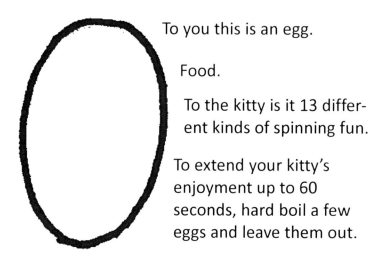

To you this is an egg.

Food.

To the kitty is it 13 different kinds of spinning fun.

To extend your kitty's enjoyment up to 60 seconds, hard boil a few eggs and leave them out.

The empty paper towel tube is also a good toy. Your cat will enjoy many, many seconds batting it around.

Things left on the bathroom counter also belong to the kitty by default. Your ~~drugs~~ medications are fair game, especially if the pills rattle in the bottle.

Your stabby thing...not a good toy

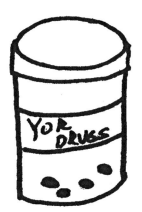

Pill container with 4 pills: good toy

(tape it closed, though. Your kitty only wants to get high on kitty crack.)

((Better yet, take the pills out and replace them with popcorn kernels.))

Look, we lick them when you're asleep anyway

There's no point in getting all bent if we play with them. They're fun to carry around, and they leave the kitty with minty fresh breath. Just wash it off before you use it again, just in case it got dragged through the litter box.

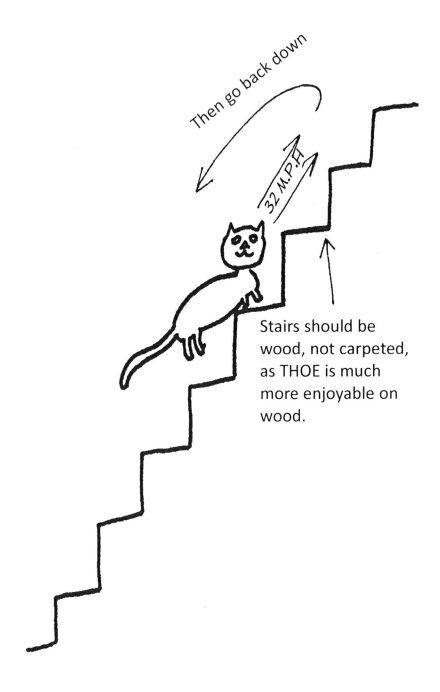

Then go back down

32 M.P.H

Stairs should be wood, not carpeted, as THOE is much more enjoyable on wood.

If there are two or more kitties in the house, the kitties may occasionally stoop to amusing each other. Often, this includes a rousing game of *Thundering Herd of Elephants* (aka THOE), during which they run at high speeds throughout the house. This game is often mistaken for simple chasing of each other, in which one kitty is trying to kill the other.

THOE is typically played at 3 a.m. in houses with wood floors and stairs, because this gives the kitties the best accousticle feedback for their game, and they know that whichever kitty makes the most noise wins. There's no point in getting upset about this; you're the one who wanted more than one kitty, and *THOE* is part of a kitty's DNA. Consider it to be good exercise for your furry friends, and go back to sleep.

If you only have one kitty and he tries playing *Thundering Herd of Elephants* by himself, you should probably get out of bed to play it with him. This will be good for his self esteem, and it will be a bonding experience for both of you.

Plus, you could use a little exercise, too.

Seriously.

Similar to THOE is a game called *What's That? Timmy's Down The Well?* This is especially fun, does not take long, but will require your participation.

This is how it goes: while you are in bed, one kitty will run up the stairs, much like he would in *THOE*, and he will jump on the bed and meow at you.

"Meow! Meow meow meow meow meow!"

And then he will run to the top of the stairs (or down the hall if you're so mean you don't have stairs for him) where he will again meow.

"Meow! Meow meow meow meow meow!"

Since he knows you're not really paying attention, he will run back to the bed and meow more insistently. "Meow! Meow!Meow!Meow!" and this is when the kitty who stayed downstairs will begin to wail "Meeeeooooooow! Meeeoooooow...*owwww!*" and then you will think "Something is wrong! The other kitty is hurt!"

Jump out of bed and run downstairs to make sure the other kitty is not dying. Both kitties will run ahead of you and into the kitchen, where you reward them with crunchy treats for their cleverness. Face it, they got you, they win, they get treats. If you don't give them treats...poop, toothy death, whatever suits their kitty whims.

The bathtub is the perfect place for a kitty to play hockey. Be sure to have several bottle caps on the edge of the tub for him to have at his disposal, as they make excellent hockey pucks. Do not complain if he plays at four in the morning because he is keeping himself amused while your lazy whahoozit is in bed.

Feathered toys are greatly appreciated by your cat. A simple stick and string with several feathers tied to the end will give your kitty many hours of stalking enjoyment. Your job is to make the feathers move, and you may not complain if the kitty takes forever to finish his game.

If you wish to not play feather toys with your kitty, then get him some feathers that are still attached to the source. He'll amuse himself, and you can go back to watching *American Idol*.

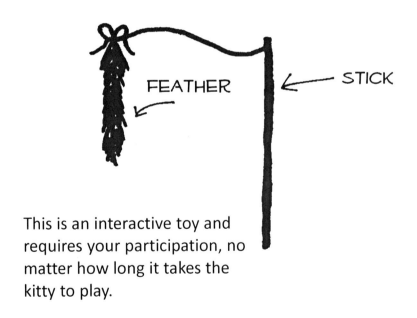

This is an interactive toy and requires your participation, no matter how long it takes the kitty to play.

Cats can be taught to play fetch with little toy mice. This will provide you with many hours of amusement as he chases it down and brings it back for you to throw again and again and again...and again. However, the game is much more exciting with real live mice. Get three or four, and watch your kitty wet himself with excitement.

Mousie. Good toy.
Live mousie. Better toy.

If the kitty finds an unintentional real mouse, there's no getting mad at him for hunting it down and doing to it what cats will do to mice. The proper responses are "Good job!" and "Thank you!" because chances are, he saved half for you.

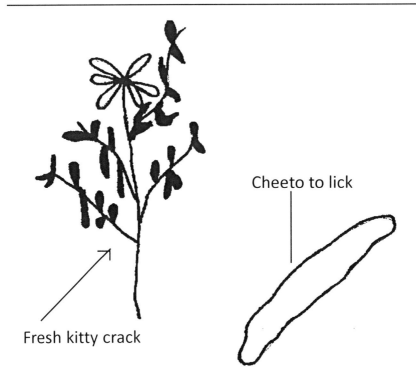

Cheeto to lick

Fresh kitty crack

Kitty crack is an important part of your cat's life. It must be replenished frequently; ideally you will grow fresh catnip and dole it out daily, but failing that, replace kitty crack toys at least twice a month so that your kitty can enjoy a high untainted by stale nip. Oh, and buy some Cheetos. After playing with kitty crack, a Cheeto is a welcome thing. Your kitty will lick it and gnaw on it and then bat it about so that it, too, becomes a toy. A wet, sticky toy.

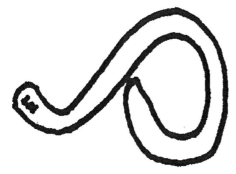

You know those ring thingies off the milk cartons? Don't throw them away. They smell like milk, and your kitty will enjoy chewing on it and batting it around on the floor.

He will lose it in 3.12 minutes, so hurry up and drink the next carton so that there will be another milk ring forthcoming. Bascially, it's a free toy, and we all know people are cheap, so you both win.

Bottle cap.
Another good toy.

Peanut in the shell.

Tons of fun, especially on wood or tile floors.

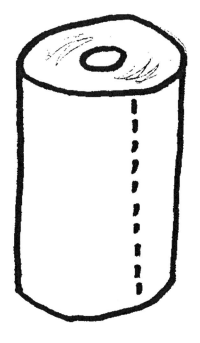

While you think of these as paper towels, useful for cleaning and wrapping around hot dogs before you stick them in the microwave, your cat finds a roll of this to be a wonderful device to scratch. While scratching, he is pretending to be a mighty hunter. You should encourage this, because otherwise he will use your leg.

When the kitty has destroyed his papery prey, don't think of the result as a mess. It is:

> A) Remains. Either eat them or bury them.

> B) Redecorating. *Devine Feline Design*. Take pictures, because HGTV might be calling.

If HGTV shows up, your kitty might get very, very rich, and then you'll be sorry if you just weren't nice enough to keep him stocked in decorating supplies.

This is not just your shoe. It is also a cat toy.

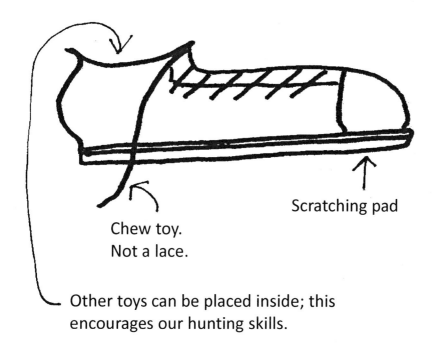

Chew toy.
Not a lace.

Scratching pad

Other toys can be placed inside; this encourages our hunting skills.

Please do not bore the kitty with deep sighs and whining that ends with "But they cost me sixty three hundred dollars!" It is not the kitty's fault that you have no self control when it comes to paying for foot wear.

Start shopping at discount stores, and let the kitty play. His play is more important than you feeling like you're stylin' in your overpriced, really ugly shoes.

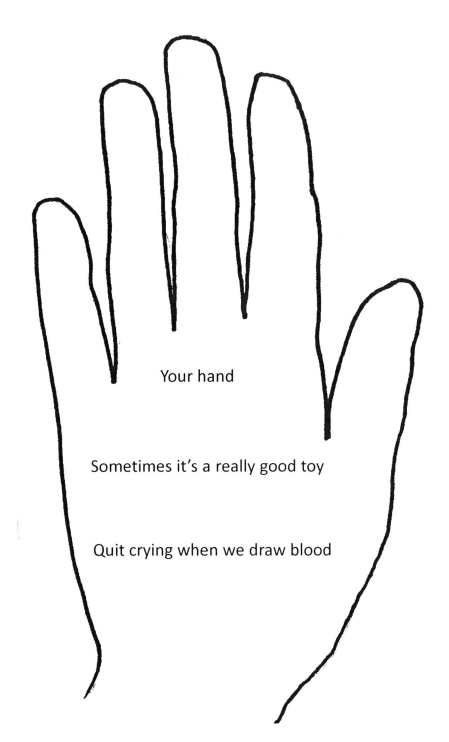

Your hand

Sometimes it's a really good toy

Quit crying when we draw blood

Everything is a toy.

Here is another blank page for you to scribble notes upon. Or draw a picture. Some of you learn better through pictures.

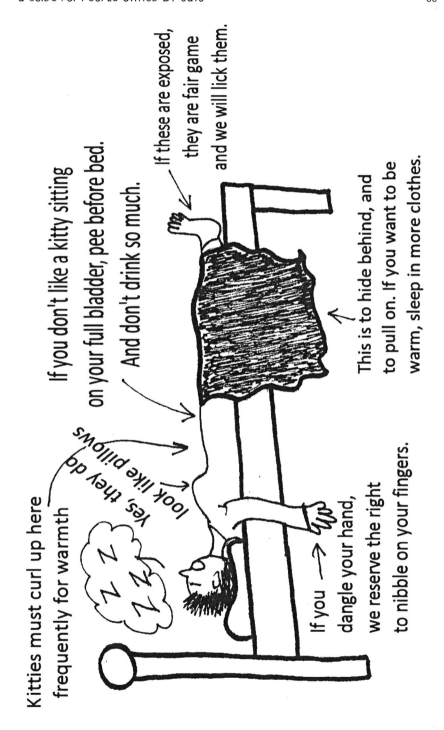

If these are exposed, they are fair game and we will lick them.

If you don't like a kitty sitting on your full bladder, pee before bed. And don't drink so much.

This is to hide behind, and to pull on. If you want to be warm, sleep in more clothes.

Yes, they do look like pillows

Kitties must curl up here frequently for warmth

If you → dangle your hand, we reserve the right to nibble on your fingers.

On Sleeping

Sleeping is over rated; you get enough sleep at night, so when the kitty wakes you up, it's for your own good. However, when the kitty is asleep, you must maintain a level of quiet acceptable for napping purposes. Cats require 16-20 hours a sleep every day, and it is your job to assure the kitty is not interrupted.

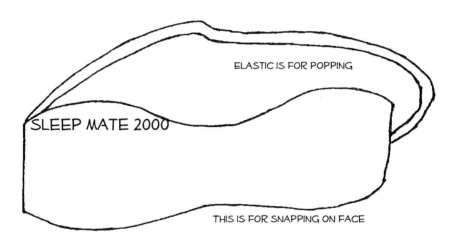

ELASTIC IS FOR POPPING

SLEEP MATE 2000

THIS IS FOR SNAPPING ON FACE

If you sleep with some fancy-schmancy thing covering your eyes to block out the light, the kitty has the right to wedge his paw under it, lift, and then let it snap back to your face in order to wake you up in the morning. Kitties are hungry, even when you want to sleep in.

It is always funny to have sixteen pounds of cat dropped onto a person's face in the morning; there's no point in getting upset about it. Part of a person's job is amusing the cat, and the cat thinks it's really funny.

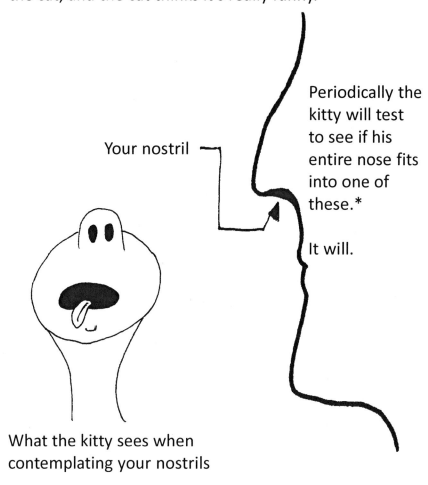

Periodically the kitty will test to see if his entire nose fits into one of these.*

It will.

Your nostril

What the kitty sees when contemplating your nostrils

Waking a person up in the morning is a devine feline right, and sometimes it involves a little nose-in-nose action.

*Especially if your nose smells really gross

If a kitty learns to curl his paw into a tiny fist and then punches you in the eye to wake you up, the proper reaction is "Well aren't you a clever kitty!" It is not "What the f...??!" [insert your favorite fun word here]

If a kitty wakes you up by bouncing on your bladder, don't get mad at the kitty. It's your own fault for drinking so much before bedtime. Drink less, and pet the kitty.

NEWSFLASH: Ladies, yes you *do* look like a bed, and yes those *do* look like pillows. It doesn't matter if your nipples invert; they're comfortable, and while you are trying to sleep I am going to curl up on you and set my head on one of them. You might as well get used to that.

You are warm-blooded; if the kitty is cold he is going to curl up on top of you while you are sleeping. There is no point in getting upset about this, and complaining that you can't roll over is a wasted effort. It's your fault for not turning the warm air blowing thingy up higher. Keep the kitty warm, and go back to sleep.

The bed is a wonderful landing surface; be sure to place tall bookcases or dressers, or even a carpeted climbing tree, near the bed. Your kitty will promise to not jump off of any of these and onto you while you sleep. Really. He'll even pinky swear.

It is a scientific fact that clean sheets create a feline magnetic force. Therefore, when you are making the bed, the kitty cannot help the fact that he is sucked into the bed sheet vortex. Do not get upset by his apparent willingness to help you change the sheets. He can't help it any more than you can help gravity. And FYI, gravity is obviously doing a hefty number on your boobs. (Don't think I'm not talking about you, too, mister...)

Do not tickle the paws of a sleeping kitty, He will twitch, and that is *not* funny. It's not. If you persist in doing so and you wake the kitty up, he gets to whap you across the face with his mighty paw 23 times.

If you are sleeping and the kitty jumps up on the bed to sniff your face and his whiskers tickle you and wake you up, well, that's perfectly all right. Pet the kitty, and tell him he's a good boy, and then go back to sleep.

Setting Up Your Bedroom

Place a tall bookcase next to the bed.

Your kitty likes to climb and jump, and the bed makes for a nifty trampoline.

Or get a very tall kitty tower. That works too.

Or both. If you love your kitty, you'll get both.

Somewhere in full view of the bed you need a TV, and it should always be tuned to *Animal Planet*.

Note there are no curtains.
The kitty doesn't like curtains.

Place the
bed under
a window.
The kitty
likes to
look out-
side.

Cup of
ice water

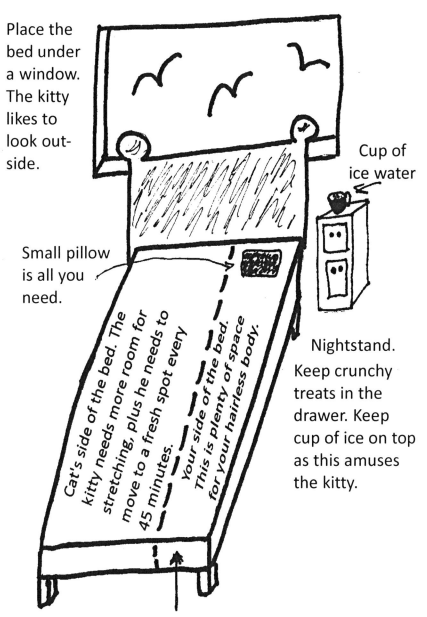

Small pillow
is all you
need.

Cat's side of the bed. The kitty needs more room for stretching, plus he needs to move to a fresh spot every 45 minutes.

Your side of the bed. This is plenty of space for your hairless body.

Nightstand.
Keep crunchy
treats in the
drawer. Keep
cup of ice on top
as this amuses
the kitty.

If you have a king size bed, you get 2% more space.

There was a lot to remember in the sleeping chapter. You really should take notes.

<u>Going To The Stabby Place</u>

P.T.U.
(Prisoner Transport Unit)

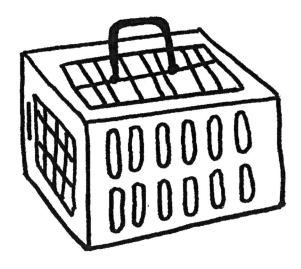

The P.T.U. is evilness typically used to force the kitty into going places he does not particularly want to go. Like the stabby place.

P.T.U. carrier

Do. Not. Want.

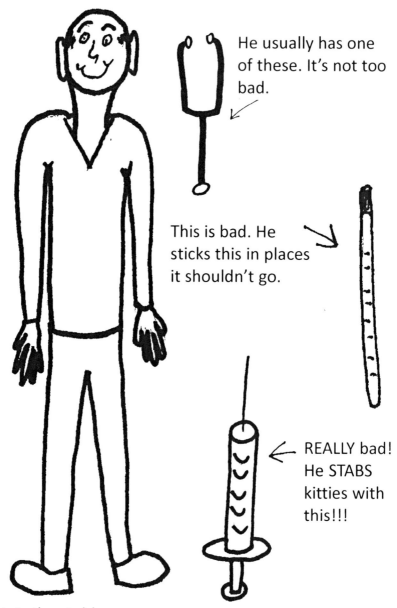

He usually has one of these. It's not too bad.

This is bad. He sticks this in places it shouldn't go.

REALLY bad! He STABS kitties with this!!!

This is the stabby guy, some-times known as "The Vet." He smiles a lot, but is is actually TeH EVIL!!1111!

When you shove a kitty into a PTU and then shove the PTU into the car, do not expect the kitty to remain silent. It is a kitty's right to complain during the entire ride,

because he knows what's going to happen and he wants to be sure you understand how unhappy he is about it. You'd complain, too, if some random stranger was going to stick things up your butt without your prior consent.

Meow? Meow? Meow? Meow?

PSYCHOKITTY

MUST SEDATE!

It is a source of pride for a kitty to have "Muse Sedate Before Exam" or "This Cat Is Psycho" scrawled across his records in bright red ink. You should be proud of your kitty for inspiring such fear, and reward him with several crunchy treats.

Sometimes the stabby place people will suggest that a cat with those proud words scrawled across his records needs to be force fed chunks of nasty tasting things called "Prozac" or "Zoloft." Clearly, the stabby people do not understand that it is *their* presence making the cat 62 kinds of crazy. These stabby people must be pooped upon. If you are not willing to do so, stand back and let the kitty work his wonders.

Medal for champion pooper.

Alternate reward
(preferred, actually)
is an entire bag of
crunchy treats.

Kitties that can poop all over the guy with the stabby
equipment, as well as the table, the floor, the wall, his
assistant, and the fake plant in the corner, should be
praised, not berated, for their behavior. Pooping this
much, and at will, is a highly developed skill.

Also, if the kitty that can poop at will makes the people
in the waiting room gag, especially with the exam room
door closed, because his poop was *that good*, he de-
serves a crunchy treat.

If he can make one or more people throw up, he de-
serves some real live fresh dead shrimp.

If the stabby guy at the stabby place tells you the kitty is fat, do not believe him. He's only trying to sell you "special food" that costs a hundred and sixty two times more than the stuff you're already feeding the kitty. The kitty is only fluffy with a sturdy bone structure, and the stabby guy is lying.

If the stabby guy tells you to stop feeding the kitty Stinky Goodness, kick him in the nads, grab the kitty, and run. Clearly he is a sadist and does not have the kitty's best interests at heart. Plus, he probably didn't really graduate from Stabby Person University. He probably flunked out. That will make a person grumpy, and he will take it out on the kitties.

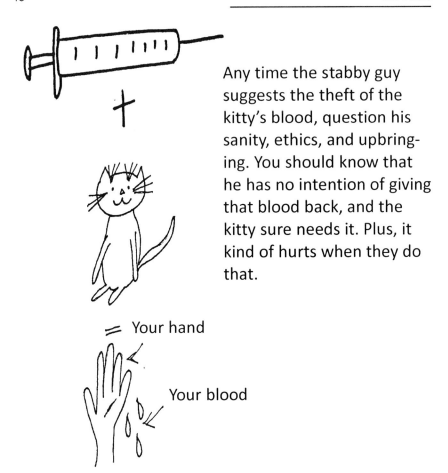

Your hand

Your blood

Any time the stabby guy suggests the theft of the kitty's blood, question his sanity, ethics, and upbringing. You should know that he has no intention of giving that blood back, and the kitty sure needs it. Plus, it kind of hurts when they do that.

Perhaps before whisking the kitty off to be spayed or nootered, you should try it on yourself first to see how you like it. If it's not at least 5 kinds of fun, let the kitty keep his fun bits. Failing that, insist he get all the fun drugs. Enough of those, and he won't really care that you zapped his manhood into dust before he even got a chance to test stuff out.

On Vomit
(Barf, Hairballs, Whatever...)

If a kitty hacks up the hairball of all hairballs, it's not nice to ask "Is your tummy empty now?"

Of course it is!

Clean up the mess, and then open up 3 cans of Stinky Goodness!

If a kitty makes an effort to throw up someplace where it's easy for a person to clean it up, then the person owes the kitty at least 5 crunchy treats.

If the person fails to reward the kitty with crunchy treats, the next time he barfs it will be in your shoes.

Super Deluxe Kitty Tower With Carpet!

Jackson Pollack Effort

The top of a carpeted climbing tower is a good place for a kitty to hock up a tummy full. Instead of being upset that he has splattered his dinner all over the floor, the walls, and quite possibly three different pieces of furniture, praise him for his Jackson Pollack efforts, then give him crunchy treats.

Just Say No!

Do not give a kitty a bath in hopes that being dunked in a tubful of water will lessen the amount of fur he ingests, which sometimes results in a hairball. You take baths, and you have hair. (Well, some of you do. The rest of you have shiny heads. Wear sunscreen and a hat.)

If you bathe the kitty, the only result will be a pissed off kitty, and a significant amount of poop on your pillow.

There are some kitties that do not mind being dropped into water. These kitties are not to be trusted. They will gnaw on you in your sleep. Plus, they will still throw up on the things that you enjoy.

If a kitty throws up, and then throws up again, and then again, and crawls into the closet to curl up in a big ball of tired, call the stabby place. The kitty will hate you for it and will later poop in the kitchen sink, but he's going to hate you no matter what, so call the stabby guy.

<u>On Bringing Home Another Kitty</u>

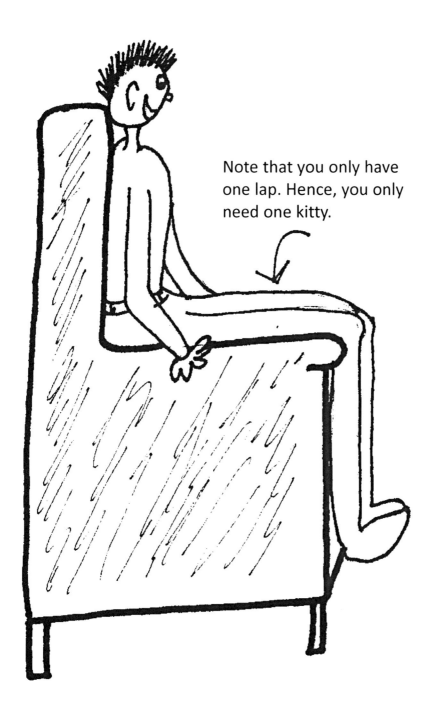

Note that you only have one lap. Hence, you only need one kitty.

Go away! We don't need your kyootness!

But I luv you!

There ~~can~~ be only one!
should

The first rule of bringing home another kitty: DON'T.

The first rule if you ignore the first rule of bringing home another kitty: all new toys, all old toys, all carpeted climbing surfaces, the first bowl of food every day, available laps, crunchy treats, and people belong to the first kitty. The new kitty will just have to learn to deal with it,

If the new kitty is deemed acceptable by the first kitty and they become best friends, then once every other week the new kitty may have the first bowl of food in the morning, and one crunchy treat.

If there are two kitties in the house and a person calls one of them "Sweetcheeks" once in a while, then don't be surprised if the other kitty takes it upon himself to determine if those cheeks really are sweet. And if they are not, the people should not get upset when the kitty who did the testing whacks the other kitty over the head with his mighty paw, because the supposedly sweet kitty only tasted like furry cat spit, and that is very disappointing.

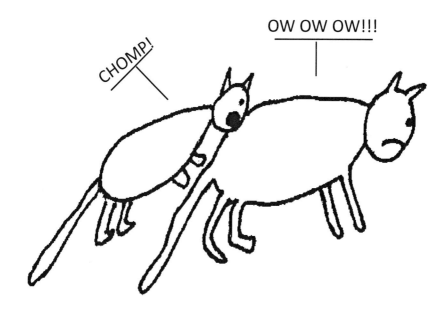

If one kitty is running down the hall, screaming, and the other kitty is running behind him with his mouth attached to the first kitty's butt, the biting kitty should suffer some kind of time-out, or maybe even get his furry little hide duct taped to the nearest solid object. Then give the good kitty some crunchy treats. Crunchy treats are like Bandaids for the kitty soul.

If you don't want one kitty
to push the other kitty down the
stairs, tell the other kitty to not
sit so close to temptation.

When a kitty jumps on your lap while you are singing to your-self and he places a paw across your mouth that means

You are not the next *American Idol*.

Remember, your kitty has very sensitive ears. Certain types of music will annoy your kitty, and you should avoid playing these. This includes opera, disco, and any music in which dogs and trucks are glorified.

If you are learning to play an instrument, practice it any-where other than the house. Your efforts bother the kitty. Heck, stab yourself in the ear with a Q-tip. That's what it feels like.

Do not complain if your kitty sits outside your bedroom door at three in the morning and sings as loudly as he can. These concerts are for your entertainment. Curl up and enjoy them. Do not tell the kitty to shut up, or the kitty will do unspeakable things in one of your shoes.

Do you want to know what real music is? The can opener. The sound of that on a giant can of Stinky Goodness is better than anything eeking out of your iPod.

CAT MATH

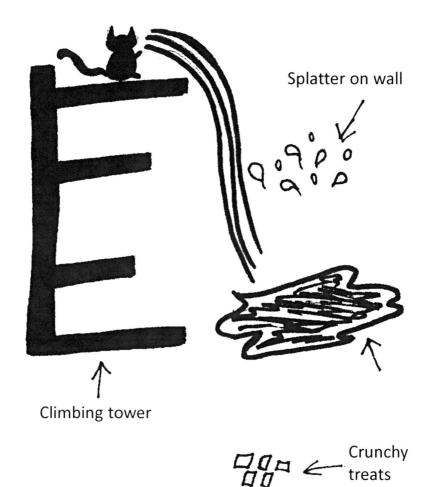

Splatter on wall

Climbing tower

Crunchy treats

(kitty + climbing tower) (barf) + wall splatter =
(exercise) (empty stomach) + art =
(fit, hungry kitty) + (talent) =
10 crunchy treats for the fit, hungry, talented kitty

First kitty

Newby kitty

3 cans   1 can

First Kitty (2 cans Stinky Goodness) + New Kitty (2 cans Stinky Goodness)

=

Upset Kitty (2 cans Stinky Goodness) + Crackhead Kitty (2 cans Stinky Goodness)

=

Hungrier Kitty + Intruder Kitty

=

First Kitty gets 3 cans + New kitty gets 1 can

=

Happy first kitty.

Problem: Person A gives the kitty 5 crunchy treats in the morning, and Person B gives the kitty 5 crunchy treats in the evening. The stabby guy says the kitty is fat and needs 15% fewer treats. How many treats should the kitty then get?

Answer: The kitty should get 6 crunchy treats in the morning and 6 crunchy treats in the evening because the stabby guy is evil and only wants to make the kitty miserable. He should be ignored and the kitty should get extra treats because you were mean enough to take him to see the stabby guy in the first place.

It's been a while since you had note-taking space. Here is another blank page for your scribbling enjoyment.

<u>ODDZ N ENZ</u>

Clothes warm
from the dryer

Kitty sleeps here

If you do not want a kitty napping in your basket of
freshly laundered clothes, then put the clothes away
before the kitty discovers them. Once a kitty sees a
basket of fresh clothes all warm from the dryer, it is his
right to curl up and shed on them.

Clean kitchen counters feel good on a kitty's tushy, so don't get all *OHMYGAWDGETDOWN!* when, within two minutes of scrubbing them sterile-clean, the kitty jumps up there and rubs his butt cheeks all over them.

We do lots of things when you're not looking. If it bugs you that much, go see your stabby guy and get a shot of penicillin.

Kitty wants to be able to get up here.
Make it happen.

Soap. Use it.

We are going to rub our butts on the counter when you are not looking, so don't get bent when you see us up there.

Open window

Fresh air

On nice days, the people should not go out and do things. They should stay home and keep the windows open for the kitties, so they can enjoy the nice breeze, too.

Seriously.

It's not fair to be out on rumbly bikes or taking long walks or hunting Big Macs when there are kitties at home waiting for fresh air.

Your pokey finger

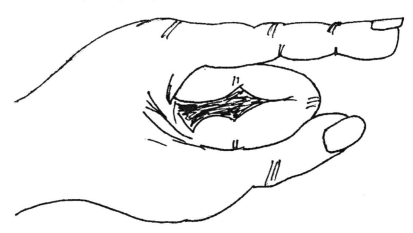

If the kitty growls at you for whatever reason (it's probably because you annoyed him) don't stick a finger in his face and say "We don't growl" because obviously, one of us does, as evidenced by how upset you are.

Mmmm...Minty...

Never presume your toothbrush has not been tested by the cat to see if it has a flavor.

Fairness in Muffins

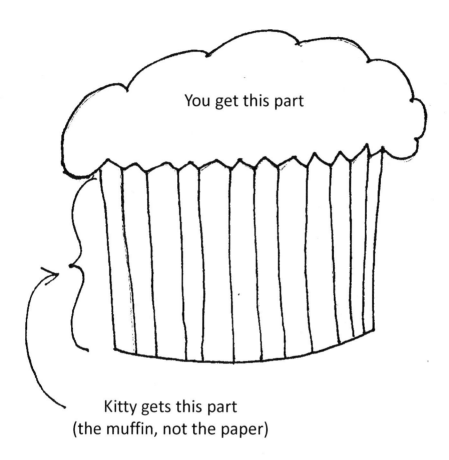

You get this part

Kitty gets this part
(the muffin, not the paper)

The first rule of making muffins: the kitty always gets a bite.

The second rule of making muffins: the kitty gets another bite.

The third rule of making muffins: if the kitty doesn't get a bite, something you like is going to meet an ugly, ugly, toothy death.

If the lid is up, that means the kitty is
allowed to play with the water.

If you are in bed and the kitty jumps up there to see you,
and rewards your existence by petting your face, don't
ask, "Why are your paws wet?" You probably don't want
to know.

Christmas trees come from nature. It is a cat's nature to climb a tree. Thusly, do not get all *No No No No* when the kitty climbs the Christmas tree.

One way or the other, we're going to reach this

Twinkle, please

Must be shiny

Leave space empty for kitty naps

This is the ultimate kitty toy.
Please leave it up longer.

Kitties enjoy sparkly, shiny things. Sparkly, shiny things hanging on a Christmas tree are a feline magnet. Do not get upset if the kitty plays with the sparkly, shiny things dangling on the Christmas tree.

If you place your dresser (or other tall object) near a light switch, and the kitty learns to turn the lights on and off, the appropriate reaction is "Good job!" even if the kitty demonstrates this talent at 3 a.m.

Paw-on Paw-off
The Paw-per

Birds

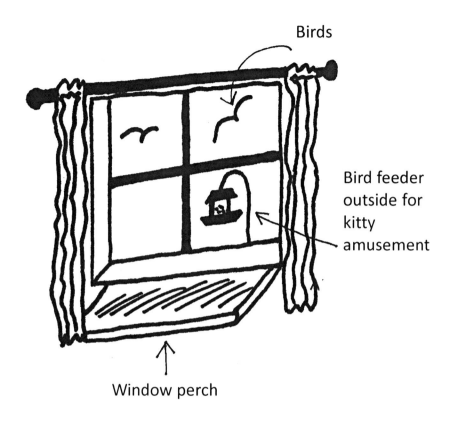

Bird feeder
outside for
kitty
amusement

Window perch

Every window must have a perch upon which the kitties may lounge and observe the outside world.

Ideally, these perches will each get a nice sun spot at different times of the day.

If none of your windows gets sufficient sun, you have two choices: buy a new house, or get your overly lazy butt outside and push the house to an angle that will put some sunshine in your kitty's existence.

When you are out hunting, this belongs to the kitties.
Leave it tuned to *Animal Planet*. We find this amusing,
enjoyable, and educational. You want smart kiitties,
don't you?

Oh, but fix it so that at 2 p.m. it automatically switches
over to *General Hospital.* Don't ask why. Just do it.

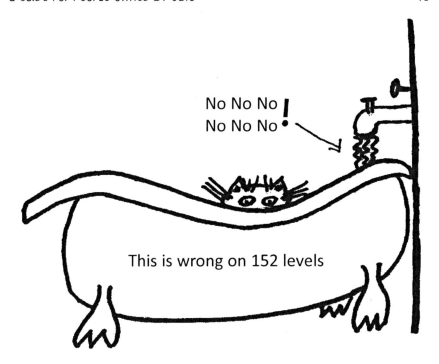

Hey. Bath boy.

Yeah, you with the tub and the urge to introduce the kitty to it.

In case you haven't noticed, kitties are very clean creatures. We have tongues, and we know how to use them. We don't need your help taking a bath! We were *born* knowing how to take a bath *all by ourselves!*

If you insist on dunking the poor, innocent cat, don't cry when you pull back a bloody stump or two.

You know what to do here

ASK THE PSYCHOKITTY

I get email. Lots of it. You got questions, I got answers.

Dear Max,

My question is a 3 tiered. I know that humans were created to serve the kitties but, is there ever a time when the kitty should throw the human "a bone," if you will, to say "thanks?"

If so, how should the kitty do this so that that human does not expect such treatment all the time?

Also, what is the best way to thank the human so that a kitty can get something out of it?

Thanks Max!

Your friend in awe, Hendrix

Once in a while a Person does something to make a kitty's day a little brighter, and they should get some kind of thanks for this. Like, for instance, when my People bought me the Supreme Commander Kitty Tower. Just from this it was obvious that they understood that I should tower above them. And when the Man put kitty platforms in most of the windows, just because he wanted me to be more comfortable as I surveyed my vast dominion, that was nice.

There are a couple things you can do to show gratitude. Catch a great big bug, and bring it to them. They like it best when you serve up a fresh one while they're in bed. They don't even mind if you eat half of it first, but since it's a gift, you should leave them the bigger half. Also, climb into their laps, stretch up, and rub your lips across theirs. It's gross, but I notice people do this together and they seem to like it and say Thanks to each other that way quite often. We can suck it up once in a while and try it. But if you just can't bring your-self to rub lips with a Person, get up there and shove your nose up one of their nostrils. This is a nice way to say thanks. Plus, if they're asleep, it will wake them up and then they can get up and give you crunchy treats.

~ ~ ~ ~

Dear Max,

Is it unusual for a cat who has just had a litter to want them on the lady's bed? I thought the mother usually hid her babies.

Katladee13

Mothers want their kittens to be happy and comfy and warm, and the bed happens to be a happy, comfy and warm place. It is not, however, your bed. It belongs to the kitties. They just happen to allow you the occasional use of it. Until the Mom Kitty is ready to allow you continued use of the bed, sleep in the bathtub. It will be good for your back.

~ ~ ~ ~

Dear Max

We have a new little brother, and he gave me herpes in my eye. How long can I get revenge on him for spreading the ick to me?

Miles Meezer

Oh man. Doooood…you have the right to infinite re-venge on the little cootie-spreader (of course, being that he's the little brother, you have a right to that anyway.) For the rest of your life, you get to do anything you want to him; try to not leave marks or bald patches, though, because that upsets the People. And oh! You want to really upset him—pin him down and give him a bath. Little brothers *hate* that!

~ ~ ~ ~

Max,

I live with a Man and a Woman and a Younger Woman. They love to snuggle and give me kitty toys and treats, *no issues there.* The problem is they're always too tired to play with me when they get home from work. Is there something that I can do to motivate them? Or do I just accept the adoration they offer and live with the rest of it?

Mrow Mrow,
Miss Lily

Truly, Miss Lily, they do not deserve you. Snuggling and toys and treats are not enough. It is their responsibility to play with you when you wish and for as long as you wish. Sadly, some People cannot get this to embed in their gray matter, and assume that kitties are solitary and do not wish interaction. They are wrong, so very wrong, and for this we kitties pay the price.

The first thing you need to do is catch a bug and play with it in front of them. Be cute—people can't resist the cute. Then when they're not really watching anymore, deposit the remains of the surely-now-dead bug on their lap. Oh, and if you can do this with a real live mouse, it works even better. Soon they will come to understand you need an outlet of some sort, and rather than deal with dead bugs and eviscerated mice, they will begin to use interactive toys with you, like feathers on a string or they'll play fetch with a toy mouse (this is degrading, fetching like a dog, but at least it gets them to pay attention.)

~ ~ ~ ~

Dear Max -

We gots a cat stroller, and we luvs it! We really had to werk hard at kissin' up to our beans, and even posted a real live petition to git signatures to support us gittin' a stroller. Problem is, now our blurpy gurl sisser gots a stroller too and she git to go strollin' WAY more than we do. That doesn't really seem fair. We werked really hard to git one, then SHE just smiles, flutters her eyelashes and . . . poof, she gits a stroller. It is even blue like ours (copycat!).

Fair is fair! We wants equal stroller time! After all - we wuz adopted furst! How do we convince our beans to let us go strollin' just as often as SHE does?

Yer buds,
Kimo & Sabi

It's the curse of the Sticky Little People. I don't know why, but adult humans turn into blabbering morons around them. Sure, they're cute, but of what use are they? They're loud, they have all these disturbing, gross, odd smells, and once they can crawl, they chase the kitty and pull his fur, and the People seem to think that's funny…but, I digress.

You must camp out in her stroller. Do not allow your people to chase you from it. When they say "No, not yours," remind them that EVERYTHING is yours, and you're only allowing them temporary use of it. If it looks like the sticky person is going to get to go out in her stroller, howl. Loudly. Pathetically. Let them know that not only is the inequality in stroller time unfair, but that it hurts your feelings, too. People don't like to hurt kitty feelings. And failing that, when one of them puts the sticky person into her stroller, rub up against the other person and meow quietly, reminding them that there are TWO big people and TWO strollers, and you can all go out at the same time like one big happy family.

If they can't understand all of your reasoning, poop on their pillows. That's only fair.

~ ~ ~ ~

Dear Max,

What do I do about a kitty who is too large to wash her own behind? Mind you, it is my fault but I still need help keeping her fresh and having good self esteem. . I don't want to embarrass her or humiliate her while washing her. How do I help her?

Jean

Um…there's no easy way. Just give her 152 crunchy treats right after washing her (warm washcloth please…it feels good even if we won't admit it), and apologize profusely, then start giving her diet kitty food. And be prepared, because when she loses some weight she'll be more nimble, and she will likely try to treat something *on your body* to a toothy death.

~ ~ ~ ~

Dear Max,

1. what is snow?

Snow is an evilness that falls from the sky to punish people for living in colder climates.

2. is snow safe to be exposed to?

In relative terms…minute exposure won't hurt, but if you stay in it too long your paws will freeze. It can be tasty, but don't eat any if it's yellow.

3. why do humans wet themselves down and rub weird smellgng stuff on them?

Because they bathe inadequately, and require aid in rending their funk to a manageable level. It rarely works. They smell like perfume AND funk, which is simply displeasing to the kitties.

4. why dont humans have fur?

Probably from generations of rubbing smelly stuff on them. It just stopped growing.

5. why do humans keep food from us and what is "a diet"?

Because they're mean. And diet…don't get me started. It's enough to point out the first three letters spell DIE.

6. what is the best kind of stinky goodness?

The best kind is the kind you don't have to work too hard to get.

7. where do you get your kitty crack?

I usually find it inside a toy or pink sock. Once in a while, though, the Woman brings in the fresh stuff, and I don't have to kill a toy to get to it.

8. is all kitty crack created equal?

Oh, no…the fresh stuff is the best!

9. is the sun really just a giant lightbulb? if so, where is the switch to turn it on?

Do you really wanna know? It's kind of scary. The sun is FIRE. But we don't wanna put it out, because then we'd all freeze and would have ice hanging off our useless nipples.

10. what is your favorite nighttime sleeping spot?
Anywhere Buddah isn't…

Munchin Hendricks

~ ~ ~ ~

Dear Max,

As I'm sure you often run into this problem; I am having difficulty with my humans. Especially my Tall Man but more recently my Lap Lady too. You see, they leave all sorts of great Kaze-toys around our house for me to play with. Things like strings, pieces of plastic packaging, band-aides, egg shells, antibiotic ointment packages, you know—cat toys! Anyhow they've been getting really mad at me. It used to just be the Tall Man but recently I think he has taken over my Lap Lady because she has this deep loud yelly voice when talking to me. Often I hear "Kaze-NO! Bad kitty!!! Why must you steal EVERY-THING". Sigh....I know, don't let it get to me but they're just SO dense and I'm really getting frustrated. Plus, I really love my Lap Lady and I can't stand to see her in such a confused unhealthy state of mind. It makes me meeze just thinking about this! I really want to help my humans over their difficulties so that all of this yelling can stop and we can have a tranquil household where instead of having to forage for my toys they actually just give them to me. Please advise wise master!!

Sincerely,
Kaze the Cat

Show them this: Hey, People, all those things, THEY BELONG TO KAZE! They are not yours, you are only being allowed the use of them, because that's how generous Kaze is. Plus, everything in the house is a toy, so what's the point in getting upset? Now, go pet Kaze and give her 56 crunchy treats, because you've obviously upset her. And realize this: if she gets too frustrated, you have things that can be pooped on, upon, and within.

~ ~ ~ ~

Dearest psychokitty

I have a question. Some may feel this is not an important enough question to include in your book. They are wrong.

Firstly, a little bit of background.

I have a brother. He smells of poo. He actually enjoys trailing poo prints all over the house. Even in the deepest of slumbers, I am harshly awakened by the dank stench of poo as my brother invades my personal space by sleeping next to me, stretching out his pooey paw prints and purring incessantly. It is disgusting.

With that in mind, my question is this:

What is the best way to get rid of a sibling? Should I offer him up for adoption on the internet, or lock him out of the house in the hope that he will move in next door?

All suggestions are welcome.

I eagerly await your advice.

Ta ta for now

HRH Yao-Lin x

I feel your pain. Buddah frequently stinks of poo, too,

but I think it's just his natural odor. I've tried pinning him down and bathing him, but it doesn't help. Sometimes I think he has poop for brains.

If you try to give him away on the Internet, your people will get mad and might not give you crunchy treats or Stinky Goodness anymore. And if you lock him out, he'll just cry until a person lets him in; and if he doesn't get that far, if something big and hairy eats him while he's out there, you'll just feel bad.

So this is what you do: find a cork. It doesn't have to be a big one. And find a tube of Super Glue. It's a very small tube and it says on the outside "PERMANENT ADHE-SIVE." Smear some of that on the cork, but be careful to not get any on your paws. Now, when the PooMeister is not looking, shove that right up where the sun don't shine. And there you go, you've stopped up the source of the offending odor, plus he won't be able to make poopaw prints anymore.

There is the small chance that he might blow up and there will be poop all over the walls, but that would only happen once, and the People will clean it up.

If the idea of that is too disturbing, you could always shove an air freshener up there. Maybe a tree shaped one. At least then his poop will smell like pine.

~ ~ ~ ~

Hi Max!

Inquiring cats want to know:

1) What's your adoption story? How did you go about deciding to adopt your humans?

I was first taken from my birth mother to the home of two of the Younger Human's friends. They did not have me very long; I was a very active kitten and curious about *every-thing,* including the inside of a recliner that they had. Long story short, I got caught in the recliner and the young people rushed me to the emergency stabby place where I cost them lots and lots of money that they did not have. That helped convince them that they really couldn't afford a kitten, and the Younger Human took me to his house, where the People were not exactly perfect, but they could afford it if I got caught inside something again. This is where I met Hank the Dog, who was a pretty decent creature as far as dogs go. So I really didn't have any say in with whom my Forever Home would be, but it all worked out. Mostly. I still have to put up with them and their People ways, and then there's Buddah Pest... I have to give some credit, when the Younger Human brought me into thouse house for the first time the Woman sucked in a deep breath and said "He's BEAUTIFUL!" So for all her faults, at least she has good taste.

2) If you grew opposable thumbs, what's the first thing you would do?

I would open every can of Stinky Goodness I could, and even cans that just LOOK like Stinky Goodness! I don't care if some of them have vegetables inside, it's just the act of being able to open the cans that would fill me with joy, and eventually lots of Stinky Goodness and canned tuna. Then I would grab a pen and start writing checks to myself, using the Peoples' checkbook, of course. They owe me, they really do.

The Furry Bambinos: Padre, Panda Bear, and Meerkat

~ ~ ~ ~

Dear Max-one-in-a-million:

I have been owned by cats before, and know each cat has its own unique personality. However, the two who currently own me (littermates, brother and sister) have a habit I've never understood.

Like all my other cats, they like to stand on my chest and "knead" me — especially what they call the skwishy parts. Then they lie on my chest. But this is the part that's strange: they lie on my chest facing my feet! Worse yet, sometimes they like to snuggle right up to my face. Having cat butt in one's face (and/or cat tail up one's nose) is NOT the most comfortable position to be in. I've tried explaining to them both that their butt is NOT their best feature, and that they are much more attractive when they face me, but all is for naught.

Max, what gives?

Caroline Hendrix

Buddah does this to the Woman; we think it stems from when he was a tiny kitten. Back then he used to be able to curl up on her shoulder, and he still kind of wants to, but he doesn't fit. So when she's lying down he gets up there and sticks his butt as close to her shoulder as he can get it. In his little pea brain he's probably sure he's curled up on her shoulder, when instead she's just getting a nice view of the glory of his former nads.

It could be that, or it could be their way of saying "Kiss my…"

~ ~ ~ ~

Dear Max,

When a kitty is *really* upset with his or her Person, which is the better revenge: Bringing a toothy death to a favored possession, or a leaving a hefty sneak-a-poo in a place designed to achieve the maximum effect?

Sincerely,
Spitty the Kitty

Both are time honored and most awesome ways to let your person know they have upset you; when something of theirs meets with a toothy death, they get all bent out of shape and start moaning "Why? Why? Why?" when if they would stop and THINK, they would know why. And a nice 7 pound poop placed well is always good, too. The problem with that is that they either discover it too soon to be really nasty, or so late that it's all dried up, which makes it lose its punch.

Now, there are other ways to show your person your displeasure. One of the funnier ones is to lick their toothbrush when they're not looking. They'll never know it, but you'll be laughing your tail off every time they use it. But I think the best one…hock a hairball into one of their shoes. This works best of all because you can get your face far enough into their shoe that they won't see the hairball, and then they'll stick their foot into it, probably while it's still all wet. They'll be grossed out for weeks, and that's good fun for the kitty.

~ ~ ~ ~

Dear Max,

My cat Mud Puddle likes to curl up on the bed with

his bum pointed my way, which is fine when he keeps his tail over it. A few nights ago he farted, so stinky it woke me up, and a few seconds later it woke him up too. He snarled at me and got down, clearly blaming the stench on my bad manners.

How can I destink my cat's farts? If they stay stinky how can I redeem myself in his eyes for disturbing him- he sleeps downstairs now.

Thanks for your help.
Tina

Deadly nether region emissions come from two sources: illness and diet. Let's presume your cat is perfectly healthy and doesn't have any cooties or little green men fermenting in his intestines. This leaves diet...whatever you're feeding him.

Now, the truth is that the best tasting food tends to produce the most stinkiness upon exit, and normally a kitty is quite proud of this. The ability to make Peoples' eyes water is proof that he is being fed the tastiest of meals, and other kitties should be very, very jealous.

The only thing you can do is feed him multiple cans of Stinky Goodness, and when he explodes in a mass of OhMyGawd, pat him on the head and say "Lucky kitty!"

Truthfully, when he ran from the bed it was because he thought *you* were the offender...or he was just mortified that his diet obviously fails all emissions tests. So to be safe, along with the multiple cans of Stinky Goodness, give him lots of crunchy treats. And shrimp.

Life with lots of crunchy treats and shrimp is a good life, indeed.

CPSIA information can be obtained at www.ICGtesting.com
Printed in the USA
BVOW011332210213

313874BV00008B/152/P